Seasons and You

WINTER

By Shalini Vallepur

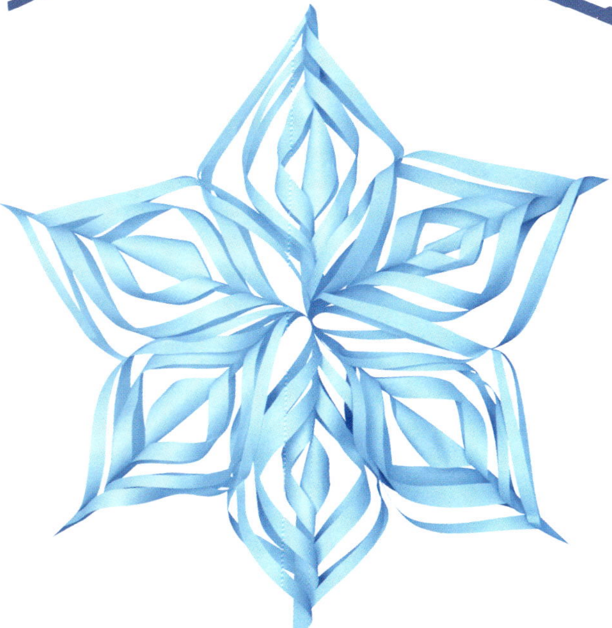

Published in 2023 by **KidHaven Publishing, an Imprint of Greenhaven Publishing, LLC**
29 East 21st Street
New York, NY 10010

© 2021 Booklife Publishing
This edition is published by arrangement with Booklife Publishing

Edited by: John Wood

Designed by: Danielle Webster-Jones

Cataloging-in-Publication Data

Names: Vallepur, Shalini.
Title: Winter / Shalini Vallepur.
Description: New York : KidHaven Publishing, 2023. | Series: Seasons and you | Includes glossary and index.
Identifiers: ISBN 9781534541412 (pbk.) | ISBN 9781534541436 (library bound) | ISBN 9781534541429 (6 pack) | ISBN 9781534541443 (ebook)
Subjects: LCSH: Winter--Juvenile literature.
Classification: LCC QB637.8 V35 2023 | DDC 508.2--dc23

All rights reserved. No part of this book may be reproduced in any form without permission in writing from the publisher, except by a reviewer.

Manufactured in the United States of America

CPSIA compliance information: Batch #CSKH23: For further information contact Greenhaven Publishing LLC, New York, New York at 1-844-317-7404.

Please visit our website, www.greenhavenpublishing.com. For a free color catalog of all our high-quality books, call toll free 1-844-317-7404 or fax 1-844-317-7405.

Find us on

IMAGE CREDITS

All images are courtesy of Shutterstock.com, unless otherwise specified. With thanks to Getty Images, Thinkstock Photo and iStockphoto. Cover & throughout – Samuel Borges Photography, Jacek Fulawka, learesphoto, Jacek Fulawka, GolubaPhoto, Mark Fearon, Nataly Studio, Art_rich, Kate Nag, ElephantCastle, Veniamin Kraskov, Ju Jae-young, Ortis, jamakosy, jannoon028, Andrei Rybachuk, Lucky_Li, timquo, pixaroma, Evikka. 4 – Gelpi. 5 – Smit. 6 – muratart. 7 – LilKar. 8 – Sakura Image Inc. 9 – Jaren Jai Wicklund. 10 – Yermolov. 11 – Alex Manthei. 12 – Julia Sudnitskaya. 13 – Galyna Syngaievska. 14 – Victoria Tucholka. 15 – bluehand. 16 – BMJ. 17 – Fufachew Ivan Andreevich. 18 – Drazen Zigic. 19 – Lisa F. Young. 20 – Elisabeth Aardema. 21 – PhotoChowk. 22–23 – Honza Krej.

CONTENTS

Page 4   **Winter!**

Page 6   **Winter Weather**

Page 8   **Brr!**

Page 10   **Plants in Winter**

Page 14   **Animals in Winter**

Page 18   **Time to Celebrate!**

Page 22   **The End of Winter**

Page 24   **Glossary and Index**

Words that look like <u>this</u> can be found in the glossary on page 24.

WINTER!

Welcome to winter! Winter is a season. Most places in the world have four seasons. Each one has different weather.

Spring, summer, autumn, and winter are the four seasons.

Winter Weather

The weather can be very cold in winter and the sun does not stay out for long. In some places it can be dark all day!

Aurora borealis

The long winter nights make it easier to see the aurora borealis.

If it gets cold enough, it might start snowing! Snowplows help to get rid of the snow that falls on roads.

Snowplow

Does it snow where you live?

7

BRR!

It can be very cold in winter. Make sure you wear lots of layers of clothing. A coat, hat, and scarf will keep you nice and warm.

Make sure you wear gloves if you play in snow! Gloves will protect your hands from the cold.

Have you ever played in snow?

PLANTS IN WINTER

Some trees will have lost all their leaves by winter. These kinds of trees usually have wide, flat leaves, but in winter the branches are <u>bare</u>.

Their leaves will grow back in spring.

Evergreen trees don't lose their leaves by winter. The leaves on some evergreen trees are called needles. The needles are long, thin, and green.

Needles

Many plants and flowers cannot grow during winter. Winter is too cold and there is not enough sunlight for them to grow.

Snowdrops are a flower that can grow during winter. They can grow even when there is snow on the ground.

What do the plants around you look like in winter?

ANIMALS IN WINTER

Some animals <u>hibernate</u> during winter when it is too cold for them. Many bats hibernate in caves or <u>roosts</u>. Most snails hibernate during winter too.

Snails stay in their shells during winter.

Hedgehogs spend winter hibernating in nests. Like other animals, it is very hard for them to find food in winter. They hibernate and wake up in the spring, when there is lots of food.

Some animals can stay warm in winter. Emperor penguins live in Antarctica where it is very cold. They stand in groups to keep each other warm.

Arctic foxes change the color of their fur in winter. Their fur gets thicker to keep them warm. It also turns white to make it harder to see them in the snow.

What animals have you seen in winter?

TIME TO CELEBRATE!

There are lots of festivals during winter around the world. Christmas is a Christian festival that is celebrated during winter in some parts of the world.

Hanukkah is a <u>Jewish</u> festival of lights that is celebrated during winter in some parts of the world.

People light a menorah over eight days.

Menorah

19

The Amsterdam Light Festival happens during winter in the Netherlands. Everyone enjoys the beautiful lights. It can last weeks or even months.

The Hwacheon Sancheoneo Ice Festival takes place in South Korea. People go fishing in icy waters. Some people even jump into the icy water!

Do you celebrate any festivals during winter?

The End of Winter

Winter happens at different times of the year around the world, but it is usually a season that gets a little colder.

What's your favorite thing about winter?

Towards the end of winter, it starts to get a little warmer and the sun stays out for longer. It isn't long before spring arrives!

GLOSSARY

aurora borealis	colorful ribbons of light that appear in the sky near the North Pole
bare	not covered up
celebrated	to have done something special for an important event
Christian	having to do with Christianity, a religion that follows the teachings of Jesus Christ
festivals	special times of the year when people come together to remember or do something
hibernate	to sleep or rest during winter
Jewish	having to do with Judaism, a religion that began in the Middle East around 4,000 years ago
protect	to look after something
roosts	places high up where animals, such as birds, can perch and sleep

INDEX

animals 14–17
clothes 8–9
festivals 18–21
flowers 12–13
hibernation 14–15
ice 21
leaves 10–11
plants 10–13
snow 7, 9, 13, 17

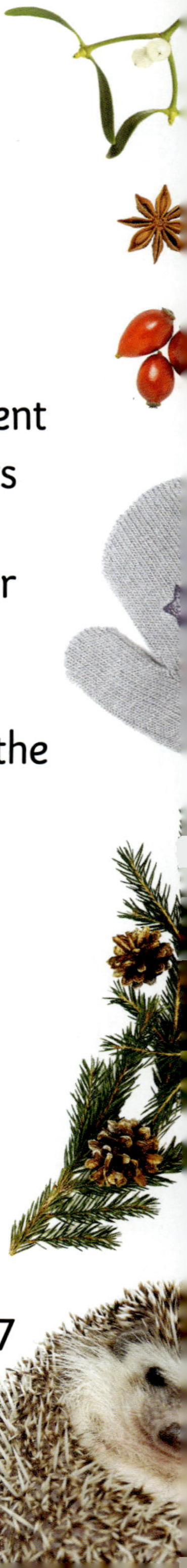